WRITTEN IN LIGHT

WRITTEN IN LIGHT

*'Abdu'l-Bahá and the American Bahá'í
Community, 1898-1921*

by

R. Jackson Armstrong-Ingram

KALIMÁT PRESS

LOS ANGELES

Kalimát Press
1600 Sawtelle Boulevard, Suite 310
Los Angeles, CA 90025
www.kalimat.com
KalimatP@aol.com

Second Printing
Copyright © 1998 by Kalimát Press
All Rights Reserved

Manufactured in the United States of America

Unless otherwise noted, the photographs reproduced in these pages are from the collection of the National
Bahá'í Archives, Wilmette, Illinois, U.S.A.

Special thanks to the Research Department, Bahá'í World Center, for the photograph of 'Abdu'l-Bahá
reproduced on p. 3.

Library of Congress Cataloging in Publication Data

Armstrong-Ingram, R. Jackson, 1954–
Written in light :
'Abdu'l-Bahá and the American Bahá'í community, 1898-1921 /
R. Jackson Armstrong-Ingram.
p.   cm.
ISBN 1-890688-02-9
1. Baha'i Faith–United States–History–Pictorial works.
2. 'Abdu'l-Bahá, 1844-1921–Pictorial works.
3. Baha'is–United States–Pictorial works.   I. Title.
BP350.A75   1998
297.9'3'0973022–dc21   98-27349 CIP

Cover design by Daniel Cook

Book design by Judy Liggett

To Karen

CONTENTS

INTRODUCTION

The past is a strange and mysterious place. We interact with pieces of it every day: buildings we live and work in; furniture we sit on, eat at, sleep in; books that we read. But every relic of the past we touch is also in the present. It is so many years older now than it was in the past. It may be deteriorated; it may be restored. It is also in a different context. The things around it are not of a piece with any of its pasts; they make a new combination never before known. And, most importantly, the people are not there; the people who lived the past, who made it.

But the people of the last century and a half do still exist in one way. They exist in images formed by light: photographs. In these photographs they exist with their buildings, their furniture, and the tangible details of their daily life. And, if we take the trouble to really look at those images written in light, we can make the past less strange and mysterious; we can enter somewhat into those lives captured by photographic moments; we can see those people interact with each other in their world; and we can understand better the roots of our own world.

This album presents a collective portrait of the Bahá'í community of the United States during the time of 'Abdu'l-Bahá. The focus is on the community, how people were Bahá'ís together. Thus, apart from 'Abdu'l-Bahá and Shoghi Effendi, there are no images of individuals alone. Faces are put to the well-known names, but those faces appear among the not-so-well-known, the context in which our later heroes actually lived.

In selecting photographs for this collection, I have largely avoided images that have been widely reproduced and have used unfamiliar images of well-known events as much as possible. There are many photographs that are already familiar and that have been used often to illustrate books. Many of these are indeed valuable, but I have tried to broaden the materials that can be drawn on in envisioning the Bahá'í past. This portrait of the Bahá'í community is intended to be well-rounded, but it is certainly not exhaustive. There are hundreds of images available; this is only a sampling that seeks to reasonably represent the whole and to supplement what is already in circulation.

I have also concentrated on providing images of less well known special events and regular community activity. In daily life, special events are special; they do not occur all the time and our lives are mostly made up of the routine, the recurring, the ordinary. At special events we are not quite our regular selves: we are made special by the event; and we make it special by stepping out of our ordinary ways. But to get to know us means not just encountering us dressed up and on show, but also meeting us casually in our everyday lives.

One limiting factor in choosing photographs was their availability to illustrate all of the two decades in question. Some years provided a bumper crop: 1909 is amazingly well documented. Other years are more elusive. Of course 1912, when 'Abdu'l-Bahá visited America, is another bumper year, and I have included more images for that year than any other. However, the collection as a whole does cover the period 1898 to 1921.

Another consideration in selecting pictures was geography. There seem to be many more photographs surviving of the Chicago Bahá'ís than of any others. This is not surprising as Chicago was such a large and prominent community. Chicago was also blessed with some enthusiastic amateur photographers who regularly immortalized Chicago events. There are Chicago pictures here, but the scope of this collection is all of the contiguous United States during the period. So, I have tried to include images that document Bahá'í activity in each region of the country that had a Bahá'í community. I have also included a small selection of photographs representing the activities of American Bahá'ís around the world.

Another factor to consider was the quality of available images. Some historically valuable photographs were unusable because the surviving print was of such poor quality that a good reproduction could not be made. Some photos were simply out of focus. However, I did not want to limit this family album to formal, posed photographs, so I also sought out snapshots that caught an event while it happened. This can be reflected by a lack of image clarity; but sometimes the blur of a swirling skirt, or the turning head out of focus in a crowd, can help to convey the life of the moment. It helps us to grasp that people did not just dress up for pictures, they lived real lives; and it is valuable if we can occasionally witness them outside the formal picture frames.

When there was more than one image that illustrated an event or activity, my bias was toward choosing the one with the most information known about it. Photographs are not just pictures, they are also stories. Any story is better if we know the names of the characters. So, in many instances, I have provided names to go with the faces, as well as the story to go with the picture. Many sources were used to assemble these stories, but there remain enigmas about these images. Some may be answered in the future, and no doubt some will remain mysteries that add to the fascination of gazing through these windows into the past.

As photographs were not the only visual materials produced by the Bahá'í community, I have reproduced a few examples of other images that were part of their experience of being Bahá'ís.

Finally, I have divided the presentation of this community portrait into two parts. The first is about the American Bahá'í community's relationship with 'Abdul-Bahá. The second is about the community itself. But you do not have to read the book cover to cover. Open it anywhere, find a picture you like, and let me tell you its story.

R. Jackson Armstrong-Ingram

WRITTEN IN LIGHT

ʻAbduʼl-Bahá and the American Baháʼís

O ye lovers of God! Be kind to all peoples; care for every person; do all ye can to purify the hearts and minds of men; strive ye to gladden every soul. To every meadow be a shower of grace, to every tree the water of life; be as sweet musk to the sense of humankind, and to the ailing be a fresh, restoring breeze.

–ʻAbduʼl-Bahá
to the American Baháʼí Community, 1905

As the American Bahá'í community came into being in the 1890s, there was naturally considerable fascination with the person of 'Abdu'l-Bahá. Having been taught (incorrectly) that 'Abdu'l-Bahá was to be considered the Return of Christ, the American Bahá'ís regarded him as their "Lord" and referred to him as "the Master." In 1899, a photograph of 'Abdu'l-Bahá as a young man was brought back from the first Western pilgrimage by Edward Getsinger. This thirty-year-old picture gave the American Bahá'ís their first idea of how the Master may have looked. Of course, by then 'Abdu'l-Bahá was a middle-aged man of fifty-five years.

The photograph is probably one of a set taken in 1868 when Bahá'u'lláh and his followers were to be sent from Adrianople (Edirne) to 'Akká. This is the same set of photographs from which Western Bahá'ís were later able to see pictures of Mírzá Mihdí, 'Abdu'l-Bahá's younger brother (p. 94), and the photograph of Bahá'u'lláh. This picture of 'Abdu'l-Bahá was widely reproduced in many forms—from a tiny, button-sized version on a lapel pin to large, framed versions for the parlor wall.

Early American Bahá'ís who visited the Holy Land on pilgrimage came to see 'Abdu'l-Bahá and to pray at the Sacred Shrines. They brought cameras with them and took pictures of 'Akká, Haifa, and Bahjí. However, 'Abdu'l-Bahá would not permit his photograph to be taken. This may have been because he wanted to focus attention on Bahá'u'lláh, rather than encourage the attention being paid to himself.

In 1903, Helen Coles was so insistent that she be allowed to take his picture that at last 'Abdu'l-Bahá relented and said that she could photograph his hand. She did, and the picture was eagerly viewed by a select few of the believers when she returned home. It was termed "the hand that holds the world."

American Bahá'ís who could not visit 'Abdu'l-Bahá in 'Akká sent him photographs of themselves by mail, and pilgrims gave him pictures of their families. A photograph of a bride can clearly be seen behind 'Abdu'l-Bahá in this picture.

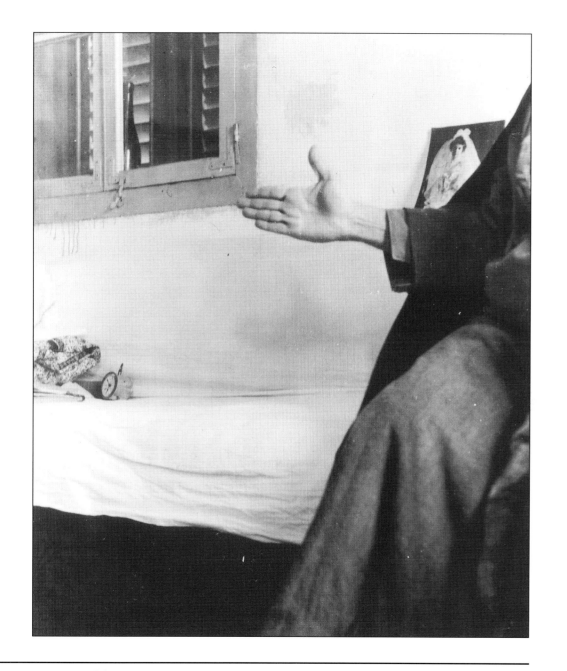

As they were not allowed to photograph 'Abdu'l-Bahá, early Western pilgrims often photographed the things associated with him: stairs he went up and down; doors he went through. In October 1909, Louise Waite photographed some interiors in 'Abdu'l-Bahá's house in 'Akká where she was staying. This picture shows her bed in the room she shared with Cecelia Harrison. Their room was next to 'Abdu'l-Bahá's, and from this window Louise Waite could see 'Abdu'l-Bahá walking in his garden and holding meetings in the summer house there. The umbrella by the window is hers.

Americans who visited 'Abdu'l-Bahá often commented on the simplicity of the furnishings in his house. As some of the other photographs in this book show, simplicity was not a characteristic of American interiors of the period. However, 'Abdu'l-Bahá's house was very typical for a notable family in Palestine at that time.

PILGRIM'S ROOM IN 'ABDU'L-BAHÁ'S HOUSE, 'AKKÁ, 1909   7

This photograph was also taken by Louise Waite in October 1909. Unfortunately, she did not always have a steady hand and the picture is not quite in focus. However, it is important as it shows the dining room where Western pilgrims ate with 'Abdu'l-Bahá and where he delivered his famous "table talks." The best known of these are in the collection published as *Some Answered Questions*. The picture on the wall between the windows is a Mashriqu'l-Adhkár design by the American Bahá'í Charles Mason Remey.

The Western pilgrims ate their meals in this room and were often joined by 'Abdu'l-Bahá for lunch or dinner. Many of them pressed flowers from the vase on this table to bring home as souvenirs. At this early period, Western women had greater access to the household than did men, and they often ate breakfast with 'Abdu'l-Bahá and his family in a different room that was furnished with divans around the walls. Western men would not join 'Abdu'l-Bahá for breakfast but would attend the morning men's meetings in the garden afterwards. These were the meetings Louise Waite observed from her bedroom window. After eating dinner in the small Western-style dining room, both Western men and Western women could join the meetings of Eastern male residents and pilgrims that were held in the later evening.

DINING ROOM IN 'ABDU'L-BAHÁ'S HOUSE, 'AKKÁ, 1909 9

When 'Abdu'l-Bahá traveled to the West (1911-13), it was at a time when new technology had made it relatively easy to reproduce photographs in print. There developed, therefore, a universal expectation by the Western press and public that newspaper articles should be illustrated. 'Abdu'l-Bahá gave in to press demands with good humor and also allowed Bahá'ís to take pictures of him during his travels. He posed with many individuals and groups to provide souvenirs of their meetings. The first of these pictures to reach America was from a series of portraits taken at a studio in Paris in 1911.

By the time 'Abdu'l-Bahá came to the United States in 1912, American Bahá'ís were eager to have photographs taken of him in American settings and to appear in pictures with him. Many of these pictures have been reproduced frequently and are well known. But no photographic account of 'Abdu'l-Bahá's relationship with the American Bahá'ís would be complete without a few reminders of that momentous visit.

One of the most notable events of the visit to America happened on Wednesday, May 1, 1912, when 'Abdu'l-Bahá dedicated the site for the Mashriqu'l-Adhkár in Wilmette. Surprisingly, this event was a very informal one, and this informality extended to the photographs. There was one arranged group photo taken after 'Abdu'l-Bahá had left to return to Chicago, but apart from that, there is only a handful of snapshots to document the occasion. A large tent had been erected on the grounds, and this photograph shows 'Abdu'l-Bahá addressing the crowd in that tent.

At the dedication of the land for the Mashriqu'l-Adhkár in Wilmette on May 1, 1912, after 'Abdu'l-Bahá gave his talk in the tent, everyone moved outside. There was an improvised ceremony during which representatives of many nations helped to make a hole by each removing a shovelful of earth. 'Abdu'l-Bahá then set the dedicatory stone in place. This photograph shows 'Abdu'l-Bahá distributing some left-over soil from the excavation as a souvenir of the event.

While staying in Chicago, 'Abdu'l-Bahá went for walks in Lincoln Park near his hotel. Bahá'ís would often wait in the lobby of the hotel hoping to see him, and as he passed through he would ask them to go along. On Saturday, May 4, 1912, one such stroll was joined by a photographer. Part of the park was also a zoo. The first photograph taken that morning was a rather formal one of 'Abdu'l-Bahá and his fellow strollers lined up across a walkway between the fenced enclosures.

After 'Abdu'l-Bahá gave permission for the first formal group photograph in Lincoln Park Zoo on May 4, 1912, he allowed some other posed pictures. The photographer then grew bold enough to start taking candid shots. This photograph shows 'Abdu'l-Bahá looking down into the polar bear's enclosure. The boy beside 'Abdu'l-Bahá also seems to be fascinated by the bear, but the expressions of the people just behind him tell a different story. They look as if they are more interested in the photographer.

There was a little conspiracy going on. The photographer had been asked to get a good picture of the way 'Abdu'l-Bahá's silvery hair curled from under his turban and flowed onto his dark robe, and 'Abdu'l-Bahá's position watching the bear showed this to advantage. Just after this picture was taken, the people behind 'Abdu'l-Bahá tip-toed back to allow the photographer to set up his tripod and focus for a time exposure to ensure a really clear shot of his white hair. 'Abdu'l-Bahá seemed to be completely engrossed in watching the polar bear, but just as the photographer took up the bulb to open the shutter, 'Abdu'l-Bahá turned round with a laugh and tapped him with his walking cane, foiling the little scheme.

On Sunday, May 5, 1912, 'Abdu'l-Bahá met with the children of the Chicago Bahá'í Sunday School. He talked individually to each child and gave them each, as a momento, an envelope with petals from flowers that had been in his room. After the meeting, he took the children into Lincoln Park. In the ensuing photo session, some of the best known photographs of 'Abdu'l-Bahá in America were taken. The photographer was A. C. Killius of Spokane, Washington. This is a rare version of one of these well-known pictures.

After having a group photo taken with the children, another was taken with both the children and the adults who were present. Several of the children can be clearly seen to be holding their envelopes, and just as clear is the Coca-Cola sign through the trees. In the versions of this photograph that were published at the time, fine ink lines were drawn on it to look like more twigs on the tree and to obscure the sign.

The woman just below the Coca-Cola sign with the pale headscarf is Grace Robarts. 'Abdu'l-Bahá was staying in a hotel where he had a complete apartment, and Grace Robarts was primarily responsible for his housekeeping. She is holding the basket that had contained the children's envelopes and which has more flowers from 'Abdu'l-Bahá's room. He had asked for extra flowers to be brought down to the children's meeting in case there were not enough envelopes ready. The woman behind Grace Robarts who is looking at the flowers is Louise Waite who helped with 'Abdu'l-Bahá's housekeeping in Chicago and who prepared the envelopes.

Shortly after 'Abdu'l-Bahá's arrival in America, a commercial newsreel company asked to film him. Moving pictures were not always considered very respectable in 1912, and it rather upset some of the Bahá'ís that 'Abdu'l-Bahá agreed. The company filmed a brief sequence of him outside the Hotel Ansonia.

Once the precedent had been set, some Bahá'ís thought it would be a good idea to make a longer film. 'Abdu'l-Bahá agreed, and after several delays due to bad weather, the film was made on Tuesday, June 18, 1912, in the garden of Howard MacNutt's home at 935 Eastern Parkway, Brooklyn. A few scenes from the film were printed as stills. This one shows 'Abdu'l-Bahá with his interpreters standing behind him and a group of children in the reception line. A recording of 'Abdu'l-Bahá's voice was also made, and it was sometimes used as a companion to this film.

On Saturday, June 29, 1912, 'Abdu'l-Bahá hosted a "Feast of Unity" on the grounds of Roy Wilhelm's house in West Englewood, New Jersey. As people gathered for the event, 'Abdu'l-Bahá rested at the Wilhelm home, mostly sitting on the porch. This photograph shows him there with a small group of Bahá'ís. The man on the right of the picture wearing the polka-dot bow tie is Roy Wilhelm. The woman standing behind 'Abdu'l-Bahá with the tea tray is Lua Getsinger.

Lua's appearance in black-and-white photographs is misleading. Compared to many of the other women, she looks as if she is very dowdily dressed. Since her youth, Lua had been "artistic" in her choice of clothes, rather than simply wearing the standard fashions of the day. When 'Abdu'l-Bahá asked her to travel in the East for him, he suggested that she should dress in a less conspicuous way. She designed a form of dress that she continued to wear after her return. When she came back to America, other women liked her clothes and asked 'Abdu'l-Bahá if they could dress the same way, but he discouraged this.

Although black-and-white photography makes her clothes appear dull and uninteresting, in fact their color was a beautiful, deep shade of blue. Also, her dresses were not made of a single fabric, but had inset panels and trimmings of silk and velvet in the same shade of blue. Her hat and silk chiffon veil were the same color. With most of the women around her at many of these Bahá'í gatherings dressed in white or shades of grey, the effect of this mass of deep blue with its subtle shifts in texture, set against her pale skin and simply arranged hair, must have been quite striking.

The "Feast of Unity" hosted by 'Abdu'l-Bahá at West Englewood on June 29, 1912, was attended by over two hundred people. 'Abdul-Bahá had invited them as his guests to set an example of hospitality and to encourage unity among the Bahá'ís. In this photograph we see a few of them trampling the meadow flowers and enjoying 'Abdu'l-Bahá's company.

Just as the feast got under way, it seemed that it would be ruined by a rainstorm. Black clouds boiled up, thunder clapped, and large drops of rain fell on the tables. The guests began to run for cover. Juliet Thompson, who was there, records in her diary what happened next:

"The Master rose calmly and, followed by the Persians, walked out to the road . . . I saw Him lift His face to the sky. He had gone a long way from the house; thunder still crashed and the clouds rolled frighteningly low, but He continued to sit perfectly motionless, that sacred and powerful face upturned to the sky. Then came a strong, rushing wind; the clouds began to race away; blue patches appeared above and the sun shone out. And *then* the Master rose and walked back into the grove. *This I witnessed.*"

On his way from Chicago to California, 'Abdu'l-Bahá stopped for a few days in Minnesota. While in Minneapolis, he gave a talk at the home of Albert Hall where he said: "Man must spiritually perceive that religion has been intended by God to be the means of grace, the source of life and cause of agreement. If it becomes the cause of discord, enmity and hatred, it is better that man should be without it."

This photograph was taken on September 19, 1912, in Loring Park, Minneapolis. The group includes Fred Mortenson, a Minnesota Bahá'í who had earlier traveled "hobo-style" on the trains from Cleveland to New Hampshire to see 'Abdu'l-Bahá at Green Acre. 'Abdu'l-Bahá had then invited him to spend a week as his guest in Malden, Massachusetts. Also in the group is Mrs. Herrick who was not a Bahá'í but who entertained 'Abdu'l-Bahá for afternoon tca. Mrs. Herrick was the sister of Edith Sanderson, a Bahá'í who lived in Europe and the Middle East and was involved in a number of translation projects for 'Abdu'l-Bahá.

Standing behind 'Abdu'l-Bahá from the left are: Dr. Homer Harper, Dr. Ameen Fareed, Kaukab McCutcheon, Ahmad Sohrab, unknown, 'Alí-Akbar Khán, Mrs. R. D. Herrick, Fred Mortenson, and unknown.

In October 1912, 'Abdu'l-Bahá traveled to California. On Tuesday, October 8, he spoke at Leland Stanford Junior University in Palo Alto and lunched with David Starr Jordan, the university president. However, he also made time for a less exalted member of the university. This photograph shows 'Abdu'l-Bahá being interviewed in the street outside the university by a reporter for the student newspaper.

On October 7, 1912, 'Abdu'l-Bahá spoke on the importance of eliminating prejudice to the Japanese YMCA in Oakland, California. He insisted that: "prejudice is a destroyer of the foundations of the world of humanity, whereas religion was meant to be the cause of fellowship and agreement."

On October 16, 'Abdu'l-Bahá was present at the Nineteen-Day Feast held in Helen Goodall's house in Oakland, California. People had come from Oregon and Washington, and there were over a hundred there. This photograph, taken outside the house, shows 'Abdu'l-Bahá with all the people of many nationalities and backgrounds who had come to celebrate the feast with him.

The woman sitting on the ground in the left foreground with the grey hair and white lace collar is Helen Goodall. The Asian men in the group (to 'Abdu'l-Bahá's immediate left; in the front row with a child; etc.) demonstrate that the Bahá'ís had already reached into the large Japanese and Chinese communites in the San Francisco area. The man looking out of the greenery on the left is Saichiro Fugita, who would later be called to live in the Holy Land as a member of 'Abdu'l-Bahá's household.

In addition to photographs, many other kinds of remembrances of 'Abdu'l-Bahá were produced and circulated in the Bahá'í community as a result of his journeys to the West. There were medals, drawings, paintings, and statuary. Many of these were in turn photographed, and the photographs reproduced and sold.

Mr. C. W. Child, a London "cheirognomist" or "scientific" hand reader, collected impressions of the hands of the famous. In January 1913, through Miss Scatcherd, he was able to meet 'Abdu'l-Bahá, who agreed to provide hand impressions for a "reading." The impressions and the "reading" were placed in *The International Psychic Gazette*, which was published in London but was available by subscription in the United States at $1.50 a year. This magazine was well known to Bahá'ís, and during this time it featured an article on a Bahá'í topic or a talk by 'Abdu'l-Bahá in every issue.

The "reading" is as banal and obvious as any newspaper horoscope, but it does seem to have benefited from Child's familiarity with other material about 'Abdu'l-Bahá, such as the Bahá'í items featured in the *Gazette*. The article on 'Abdu'l-Bahá's hands must have been well received, nonetheless, as it was then issued as a separate booklet from which the impressions of the hands are reproduced here. Life-size copies of the hand impressions printed on art paper were also available for those who wanted to buy them for framing.

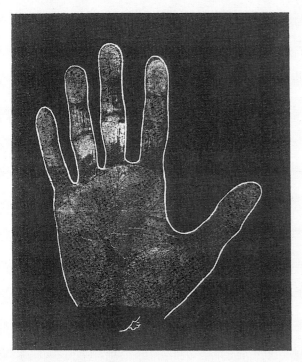

* Reduced autographed impression of the Left Hand of
THE MASTER (ABDUL BAHA)
(Impression taken by C. W. CHILD).

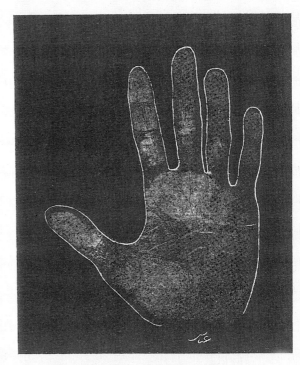

Reduced autographed impression of the Right Hand of
THE MASTER (ABDUL BAHA)
(Impression taken by C. W. CHILD).

great truths in a world of men largely given over to mammon and self-aggrandisement. The narrowing of the third, in conjunction with the strong, majestic second (middle) finger, and the sloping line of head,

---

* The triangular piece joined on the palm—so noticeable in the illustration—is from a second impression, the first not sufficiently bringing out the lines for purpose of reproduction, although giving a faithful outline and shewing the development of the hand.

bespeaks dislike of convention, love of solitude, and rare ability to penetrate and understand spiritual things.

I have shown that Abdul Baha possesses an invincible will, as evidenced by his thumbs. Attention to the placing, position, and formation of his first, index finger, will immediately disclose the fervent

When 'Abdu'l-Bahá returned home after his Western excursions, he allowed pictures of himself to be taken in the Holy Land for the first time. However, one gets the feeling that quite a few of them were taken with something of a guilty conscience, as many are from an angle of view that would have kept the photographer out of 'Abdu'l-Bahá's line of sight. There are many pictures of 'Abdu'l-Bahá's back as he walks away from the camera. This picture was taken in 1915, by George Latimer of Portland, Oregon. 'Abdu'l-Bahá is standing on the balcony of a recently completed building on Mt. Carmel.

The first World War interrupted travel to the Holy Land, and Western Bahá'ís had no new pictures of 'Abdu'l-Bahá during the later war years. The first picture they saw of him after the British forces occupied the Haifa and 'Akká area was taken in the garden at Bahjí with a British officer in late October 1918. The photograph by then Lieutenant H. E. Eckersley was sent to the United States for publication in the Bahá'í magazine *Star of the West* where it appeared in the January 19, 1919 issue.

When pilgrims started to go to the Holy Land again after the war, 'Abdu'l-Bahá allowed them to photograph him, and he again posed with groups. There are a lot of group photographs from this period. Often they were taken on the steps of 'Abdu'l-Bahá's house in Haifa, or in front of the Shrine of the Báb. Shoghi Effendi appears in a number of these pictures.

This picture was taken in the spring of 1919. Seated directly behind 'Abdu'l-Bahá are Laura Dreyfus Barney and her husband, Hippolyte Dreyfus; beside him is Shoghi Effendi. The man with the beard directly behind Hippolyte Dreyfus is 'Abbás Qulí, the Keeper of the Shrine of the Báb. The tall man with the moustache and watch-chain behind Laura Barney is Azizullah S. Bahadur, who was one of 'Abdu'l-Bahá's secretaries and translators.

To the American pilgrims who visited the Holy Land in the last years of 'Abdu'l-Bahá's life, Shoghi Effendi was known as 'Abdu'l-Bahá's grandson and one of his secretaries. His name was familiar as a translator of tablets and, like other secretaries, as a writer of "diary letters" that provided news about 'Abdu'l-Bahá and his household.

One gets the impression that Shoghi Effendi did not much like being photographed. He appears in many pilgrims' pictures from his childhood, but he nearly always looks uncomfortable and as if he would rather be somewhere else. It is noticeable that whenever he appears in a larger group photo, he is usually tucked away toward the back—but when he is in a group with 'Abdu'l-Bahá, he is placed prominently in the first row. There are a few pictures of Shoghi Effendi where he appears at ease. This is the best of them all. It was taken in 'Abdu'l-Bahá's garden in November 1919.

The American Bahá'ís not only knew 'Abdu'l-Bahá from photographs or the privilege of meeting him, they also knew him through correspondence. This photograph of 'Abdu'l-Bahá, taken in 1921, shows him signing a tablet. He is writing in the traditional way with the paper held in the left hand, the first finger of that hand providing pressure beneath the page to meet the point of the pen as it moves across the paper.

Abdu'l-Bahá's earlier tablets were signed with his initials and marked with his seal. While 'Abdu'l-Bahá was in the United States in 1912, his seal was stolen by Ameen Ullah Fareed. 'Abdu'l-Baha then instructed the Western Bahá'ís that only tablets signed with his full name in English and Persian should be accepted as authentic.

The first time he signed his name in English seems to have been in Chicago in early November, 1912, when he wrote and signed a note on a copy of the words of Louise Waite's "Song of Thanksgiving." She recalled that the Persians accompanying 'Abdu'l-Bahá were amazed, as they had never seen him write his name in English characters before. He signed his name this first time "abdul Baha" with a very small "a" and a capital "B." Later he signed tablets "abdul Baha abbas" with two small "a"s and one large "B."

This tablet is written in 'Abdu'l-Bahá's own hand and was signed by him. It was originally published in *Star of the West* (October 16, 1915). Addressed to the American Bahá'ís, it praises Lua Getsinger's teaching efforts in India.

٩

ای جناب الهی ... به لئة آنکه در هندوستان نشو و نما کنید طیبه محبت الله مشغول بود

حال بصفوت اوراک برجعت میکند درحق او رعایت مجری دارید زیرا

درعهد محبت ... و در رفقه در سفر هندوستان بسیار زحمت

... و سرور و از محبت ... عبدالله عباس

abdel Baha abbas

The Bahá'í Community

> . . . 'Abdu'l-Bahá experienced a joy so vehement that no pen can describe it, and thanked God that friends have been raised up in that country who will live together in perfect harmony, in the best fellowship, in full agreement, closely knit, united in their effort . . . they must do all they can to strengthen this compact, for such an alliance for brotherhood and unity is even as watering the Tree of Life: it is life everlasting.
>
> –'Abdu'l-Bahá
> to the American Bahá'í Community, 1905

By the late 1890s, Bahá'í communities were becoming established in a few towns and cities in the United States. This photograph of the Bahá'í community of Kenosha, Wisconsin, was taken around 1898. There is another well-known group photograph of the Kenosha Bahá'ís taken in 1897 that has been reproduced in a number of books. This is a different photograph, but it was taken in the same studio in front of the same backcloth.

In both photographs, many of the Bahá'ís are wearing small bouquets of spring flowers. This likely indicates that the photographs were taken at Easter. Many early Bahá'í communities celebrated Easter and Christmas, and the Kenosha Bahá'ís may have had these photographs taken to provide an annual picture of their community in its Sunday best.

Edward Getsinger (second row, fourth from left) was a member of the first group of Western Bahá'ís to visit 'Abdu'l-Bahá in 'Akká. The pilgrims began to arrive in the last weeks of 1898. This picture was taken in a photographer's studio in Haifa on March 21, 1899, the Bahá'í New Year.

Sitting in the middle of the second row is Ibrahim Kheiralla who, along with Anton Haddad, was the first to teach the Bahá'í Faith in America. To Getsinger's left is Mishkín Qalam, the famous Bahá'í calligrapher, with spectacles and long hair worn in the style of a Sufi dervish.

أخذت في حيفا يوم النيروز سنة ٤٧ من الإشراق في فوتوغرافخانه سنة ١٣١٦

The first Bahá'í teacher who was sent to the United States at 'Abdu'l-Bahá's instruction was 'Abdu'l-Karím-i Tihrání, who arrived in New York in late April 1900. In this formal photograph, Thornton Chase is seated beside Tihrání. To Tihrání's left is Lua Getsinger. The men in the back row are (left to right): Anton Haddad, a Lebanese believer and the first known Bahá'í to have set foot in America; Mirza Sinore Raffie, Tihrání's interpreter who traveled with him in America; Arthur Pillsbury Dodge, a prominent New York Bahá'í; and Edward Getsinger, Lua's husband.

After arriving in New York, 'Abdu'l-Karím-i Tihrání traveled on to Chicago, which had the largest Bahá'í community in America. In this photograph he poses with a large group of Chicago Bahá'ís of all ages. The framed Greatest Name hanging on the porch post shows that, as early as 1900, this symbol of Bahá'í identity had already become familiar and was being included in American photographs.

Not all of Tihrání's meetings with the Bahá'ís were formal. This is one of a series of photographs taken at a picnic held on the farm of Chester Thacher near Chicago in the summer of 1900. Thacher was a prominent early Chicago Bahá'í. There were a number of photographs taken at this picnic, and it seems to have been a particularly relaxed and enjoyable event. Some of the younger people had brought bicycles to ride, and their elders felt comfortable enough with one another to lounge on the grass and get better acquainted.

After Tihrání, 'Abdu'l-Bahá sent his brother-in-law, Mírzá Asadu'lláh, to America as the second in a series of Persian teachers who were given the task of guiding the new Amcrican believers. He arrived in November, 1900, and stayed until May, 1902. This photograph shows Asadu'lláh, in the white fez, with a large group of Chicago Bahá'ís. To his left is Mirza Sinore Raffie.

The large piece of calligraphy supported by the two men standing on the roof of the porch reads: 'Abdu'l-Bahá, the Center of the Covenant. It was probably written by Mishkín Qalam and was one of the pieces brought back from 'Akká by Edward Getsinger.

WITH BAHÁ'ÍS, CHICAGO, C. 1901

ASADU'LLÁH WITH BAHÁ'ÍS, CHICAGO, C. 1901   59

On August 16, 1902, the young Carl Scheffler and Albert Windust, who were to go on to spend decades serving on Bahá'í institutions and to have a prominent role in the development of the American Bahá'í community, posed for this photograph with Ameen Fareed, the son of Mírzá Asadu'lláh and the nephew of 'Abdu'l-Bahá's wife, Munírih Khánum. He had come to the United States to translate for his father and to study. Looking at the condition of the bicycles they are posing with, it seems amazing that any of them survived long enough to do anything.

This photograph of the architect's drawing for the planned Bahá'í House of Worship in Ashkabad, Russian Turkmenistan, was sent to the Chicago Bahá'ís in early 1903. Seeing it helped inspire Chicago to begin plans for their own building. This photograph was published in a number of newspaper articles at the time. As is often the case with architects' drawings, the building as built in Ashkabad did not look exactly like its original design.

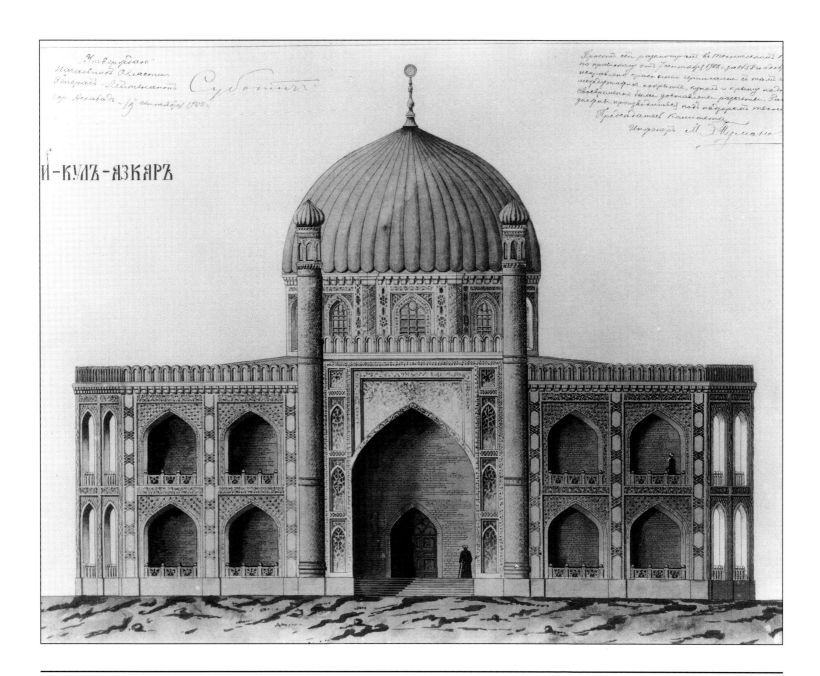

И-КУЛЪ-ЯЗКЯРЪ

Fruitport was not far from Muskegon, Michigan, from which a regular ferry service ran to Chicago. Because of the ferry across Lake Michigan, this area became popular as a summer resort that allowed Chicagoans to get away from the heat of the city. Corinne True had a summer home in Fruitport, and a small but vigorous Bahá'í community developed there. This photograph was taken in 1903 and is reputed to be the first photograph taken of the believers there. In addition to the Fruitport Bahá'ís, the picture includes members of the Tobin family from Chicago. I think the photograph was likely taken by Corinne True.

From left to right, those standing are Mrs. Christine Peterson, Nels Peterson (who is holding Agnes Peterson), John Tobin, Harold Tobin, Frank Nash, and Anna Peterson; seated are Florence Bishton, Maggie Hendryx, Mrs. Nettie Tobin, and Alice Bishton; the children in front are Edna and Henry Peterson.

This photograph shows a Naw-Rúz celebration in Washington, D.C., c. 1905, being held in a typical American middle-class home of the period. Among all the bric-a-brac, one can see some of the things that American Bahá'ís added to their homes to demonstrate their new faith: the elaborately framed lithograph of 'Abdu'l-Bahá as a young man and the Greatest Names on gold and red patterned backgrounds designed by Charles Mason Remey. Remey himself holds up a large one of these at the back of this group, and a smaller one hangs on the wall.

The only man sitting at the table is Joseph Hannen, who would become a leading advocate for racial integration in the Washington Bahá'í community despite pervasive prejudice and entrenched customs of racial segregation. We can tell this is a Naw-Rúz celebration from the plate of sprouted seeds prominently placed in front of the group. The sprouts (*sabzih*) are a traditional Persian New Year decoration.

Eva Webster Russell was a keen amateur photographer. The following two snapshots, taken around 1905 or 1906, are representative of many which were taken against the fence in the backyard of the house she shared with Dr. Susan Moody on South Hoyne Avenue in Chicago. Ameen Fareed lodged with them, and he traded off with Mrs. Russell to take this pair of photographs. The small flower bouquets pinned to their clothes suggest that this may be another Easter occasion. (See p. 48). In this photograph are, from the left, Dr. Susan Moody, Cecilia Harrison, Beatrice Davies, Ameen Fareed, and Isabella Brittingham.

For the second photograph taken on this spring day, Fareed must have pushed the button. From the left are: Dr. Susan Moody, Cecilia Harrison, Beatrice Davies, Isabella Brittingham, and Eva Russell. The locket Eva Russell is holding open seems to contain one of the miniature photographs of 'Abdu'l-Bahá as a young man. (See p. 2)

This photograph, taken around 1905, shows the home of the Davies family at 5847 S. LaSalle St., Chicago, with Mrs. Davies and her daughters standing in front. This is the kind of middle-class house that most members of the Chicago Bahá'í community lived in. 'Abdu'l-Bahá visited this house in 1912.

Beatrice Davies, in the white dress, is quite conspicuous in a number of early photographs of Chicago Bahá'ís, as she often adopts the rather wilting pose that was fashionable among young women at the time.

Attention to the Bahá'í education of children began early in the history of the American Bahá'í community. This cheerful group photograph, taken on October 14, 1906, is of the first Bahá'í Sunday School class in Chicago. Singing and music played an important role in such classes. Louise Waite wrote two of her best known Bahá'í hymns for the Chicago children's classes.

In the back row are Edward Gale, Ernest Walters, Chester Rasmusson and the class teacher, Dr. Susan Moody. In the front row are John Gale, Lillian Walters, Katherine True, and Christina Peterson.

Although large Bahá'í communities developed in such cities as Chicago and New York early in the 1900s, a great number of small communities existed in less prominent locations. This photograph of Bahá'ís and their friends was taken in Morgan Park, Illinois, by E. Fitch in August, 1907. By including the Greatest Name, they indicated that the photograph memorialized a Bahá'í occasion, perhaps a Nineteen-Day Feast.

In the front row, from the left, are Howard Ruppers, four Morgan Park children, Laurence Ruppers, and George Ruppers.

In the second row are a local boy and then the three Bowman children.

In the third row are two local young women, Mrs. Bara's mother, Mrs. Bara (formerly Mrs. Bowman), Mrs. Nellie Gorman, Mrs. E. Fitch holding Clyde Fitch, Josephine Nelson, and Mrs. Edward Ruppers holding Nina.

Standing at the back are Mr. Bara and Edward Ruppers.

ahá'í children's classes were organized in Philadelphia in May 1907. This photograph was taken in June, as a gift for Marie Watson (second from right), the class teacher.

GIFT FOR THE TEACHER, PHILADELPHIA, 1907   79

To meet the needs of the large Chicago Bahá'í community, various Bahá'í organizations sprang up very quickly. This photograph, taken around 1908, shows the members of the Young People's Society with their chaperones, Gertrude Buikema and James Woodworth.

In the seated row, the identity of the first young man and woman are not known, but the rest from the left are: Sadie Holcom, Nellie Holcom, Edna McKinney, Clara Tichson, Charles Moralius, Genevieve Davies, and Carl Scheffler.

Standing (left to right) are: Herbert Andersen, John Burma, Rudolph Ioas, Sophie Loeding, Pauline Luehr, Gertrude Buikema, Guy Comer, Beatrice Davies, James Woodworth, George Loeding, Nina Davies, and Tony Jaeger.

This photograph of those gathered at the celebration of the Feast of Ridván in Los Angeles on April 21, 1908, was taken by a photographic enthusiast who recorded on the back of the picture that it was shot at f.16 from 30 feet, with an exposure of 1 second, at 4 p.m., and under dull conditions. Unfortunately, the photographer was not so interested in recording details about the location, or the names of the people!

Most of the participants are holding flowers. It was common at early Bahá'í feasts for someone to bring flowers to hand around, just as others would bring cake or ice cream.

Corinne True's home at 5338 Kenmore Avenue, Chicago, was much bigger than the houses lived in by most Chicago Bahá'ís, so she was able to host quite large meetings. This photograph shows her (second from left) with some of those who came for the first Bahá'í national convention, held in March 1909, at which the Bahai Temple Unity was established. Some of the sessions of that convention were held in her house.

This photograph taken on September 3, 1909, shows the growth in the number of students attending the Chicago Bahá'í Sunday School since classes started in 1906. (See p. 74.) Dr. Susan Moody (third from the right in the back row) was still teaching classes, but she would very soon leave on pilgrimage to visit 'Abdu'l-Bahá in 'Akká. From there, she traveled on to Tehran to establish a medical practice in that city.

This series of group photographs taken by Eva Russell was shot at one of the regular Nineteen-Day Teas arranged by the Women's Assembly of Teaching in Chicago. This one was held at the home of Sophie Loeding, 4318 Greenview Avenue, on July 19, 1909. The Women's Assembly of Teaching complemented the all-male Chicago House of Spirituality, which was the central institution of the community.

In the first photograph, seated from the left are: Emily Olsen, Mrs. Grayson, Clara Tichson, Grace Foster, and Mrs. Watson. Of those standing, the identity of the first two young women is not known, but following are Sophie Loeding and Maybelle Thummel.

In the second photograph, seated from the left are: Wallace Agnew, Alma Albertson, Mrs. Arthur Agnew, Mrs. Schroeder, and Eva Webster Russell who must have had someone else pushing the shutter for her on this one. Standing are Dr. Susan Moody and Mrs. May.

In the third photograph, seated from the left are: Louise Waite, Louella Kirschner, Ida Brush, and Jean Masson. Standing are Christine Loeding, the hostess, and Laura E. Jones.

In the fourth photograph, seated from the left are: Mrs. Fry (Louella Kirschner's mother), Sophie Englehorn, Maybelle Thummel, Mrs. Walters' sister, and Mrs. Walters. Standing are: E. Lundberg, Mrs. Thummel, Mrs. Welenberg, and Sophie Scheffler.

This photograph was taken on December 4, 1909, when the Philadelphia Bahá'í community gathered at 6615 Havangford Avenue to welcome Elizabeth Stewart back from her pilgrimage to 'Akká. Although there are twenty-two people in this picture, not all members of the community were present. As an alternative to holding a framed Greatest Name to indicate the Bahá'í nature of the occasion, the photograph was later stamped with this symbol. Greatest Name stamps were available in various sizes and Bahá'ís used them to head letters, mark their books, and otherwise associate things, such as this photograph, with their feelings of Bahá'í identity.

In the front of the photograph from the left are: Flora E. Revell, Mrs. Elwood Revell, Ethel Revell, Walter Summers, Mr. P. Summers, Irvin Summers, Florence Hollings, Mary Revell, Mrs. William Revell, Rebecca Revell, Jessie E. Revell, and Elizabeth Stewart.

Standing from the left are: Sigurd Dahl, Mrs. H. Weyand, A. M. Dahl, Mrs. Landseidel, William Revell, Mrs. A. Fesler, Mrs. M. J. Revell, Elwood Revell, Marie Vey, and A. Fesler.

Bahai News was not the first American Bahá'í magazine, but it was the first to continue to publish for an extended period. In 1911, it was renamed *Star of the West* and was a major vehicle of communication and sharing between Bahá'ís in North America and the rest of the world. The cover of the first issue (March 21, 1910) was an instance of this sharing as it included a photograph of Mírzá Mihdí, the younger son of Bahá'u'lláh, who had died tragically in 'Akká. This photograph was one of the set taken in 1868 in Adrianople.

The copy of the photograph that was used for this cover had been sent as a gift to the Western Bahá'ís by Fareeza Khanum. It was duplicated and the copies were attached individually to each one of the first issues.

BAHAI NEWS

Vol. 1   Chicago, (March 21, 1910) Baha   No. 1

THE " PUREST BRANCH."

In reproducing the photograph of the "Purest Branch" so lovingly sent by the maid-servant of God, Fareeza Khanum, to the friends in the Occident, the following extracts from the "Life and Teachings

Lesley O'Keefe hosted the feast for the Bahá'í community of Spokane, Washington, on July 5, 1910. At this time, Nineteen-Day Feasts were often known as "Unity Feasts." Spokane held these Unity Feasts regularly. The community usually met in homes, but this time they took advantage of the perfect weather to meet on a pine-covered hillside outside town. After the feast, photographs were taken with the intention of sending copies to Persian Bahá'í communities. Many Bahá'í communities in the United States corresponded with communities in Iran and sent them photographs of events. The Persian inscription reads: Bahá'í meeting in the City of Spokane (Washington State) held in a garden for the Nineteen-Day Feast.

انجمن بهائیان شهر اسپوکان (ایالت واشنگتن) که در موقع عید نوروز ده در باغی جمع شده‌اند

The American Bahá'í community developed ties with Eastern Bahá'ís through correspondence, by exchanging community photographs and publications, and by visiting each other's communities. Eastern Bahá'í communities were not only found in the Ottoman Empire and Persia. There were well-established Bahá'í communities in the Indian sub-continent and nearby Burma. Several American Bahá'ís visited these communities in the early years of this century.

This photograph was taken in Burma in 1910, and is likely a Rangoon youth study class. Second from the left in the second row is Charles Mason Remey. Remey toured India and Burma on this trip with another American Bahá'í, Howard Struven.

Dr. Susan Moody went to Tehran in 1909, to help establish a hospital there. By the time this photograph was taken in 1913, she had been joined for some years by three other American Bahá'í women. These women were not only involved with providing healthcare, but also played a large role in helping Persian Bahá'í women establish schools for girls. One of the women they worked with was Tá'irih Khánum whose daughter is seen here having tea with the American women in a garden.

From left to right are: Lillian Kappes, who was principal of the Bahá'í-sponsored girls' school in Tehran and who also taught at the boys' school; Múhíbbih Sultán; Tá'irih Khánum's daughter, Múchúl Khánum, with her three children seated among the women; Dr. Susan Moody; Dr. Sarah Clock; and Elizabeth Stewart, Dr. Moody's nurse. Both Lillian Kappes and Dr. Sarah Clock would die in Tehran in the 1920s and were buried in the Shrine of Varqá and Ruhu'lláh, the martyred Hand of the Cause and his son.

Bahá'ís did not only get together for religious occasions. This group simply spent a summer's day having fun on the Potomac River near Washington, c. 1914.

In the middle, at the front, is Edward Getsinger. Behind him from the left are: Howard W. Blakely (not a Bahá'í), Donna Moore Blakely, Ursula Shuman Moore, and three Washington Bahá'ís whose names are not known. At the back are the children of Howard and Donna Blakely, Dudley Moore Blakely and Walter H. Blakeley. Edward Getsinger's wife was Lua Moore. Six of the ten Moore siblings became Bahá'ís.

As well as traveling east, North American Bahá'ís traveled west to bolster and encourage the Bahá'í community in Hawaii. This photograph was taken in Honolulu in 1915. In the back row (left to right) are Charles Mason Remey and George Latimer, two prominent Bahá'ís visiting from the mainland. The second woman from the right is Corinne True.

During this visit, Remey, Latimer, and True were granted an interview with Queen Liliuokalani, the last of Hawaii's monarchs. The queen was impressed by the encounter and asked for Bahá'í literature.

In the mid-teens, feasts with a Mashriqu'l-Adhkár theme started being held to increase interest and encourage contributions toward building the Mashriqu'l-Adhkár in Chicago. This photograph was taken in the Latimer home in Portland, Oregon, in 1915. As a centerpiece for the feast, Charles Mason Remey had organized the building of a simplified model of the Mashriqu'l-Adhkár in Ashkabad. The model had a wood and cardboard frame, which was then decorated with flowers and greenery. More greenery was used to suggest the gardens around the building.

As the leaves look rather tired in this picture, the photograph was probably taken the day after the feast. On the left is George Latimer; behind the table, Remey; and to the right, George's parents.

This photograph of Bahá'ís attending the Feast of Perfection on Rose Hill, Los Angeles, was taken on Sunday afternoon, August 20, 1916. Everyone in the picture would have had to hold this pose for some seconds as the panoramic camera turned to encompass the whole group. Obviously, holding the feast on a hilltop did not bring down standards, judging by the teacups and elegant clothes. The display arranged in the center of the photograph, with the Greatest Name flanked by pictures of 'Abdu'l-Bahá and Jesus Christ, clearly shows how many Bahá'ís connected their new faith to their Christian heritage.

Standing from the left are: Minnie Lou Woods, Mr. and Mrs. Woods, Beatrice Irwin, Mr. Isgrigg, Mrs. Beckett, Miss Button, Louise Waite (kneeling in the middle), Mr. Eddy, Mrs. Wagner, Dr. Clark-Smith, Mr. Alexander, Mr. Beckett, and Mr. Anderson.

Seated from the left are: Mr. Watkins, Mrs. Young, Mrs. Ditlz, Mr. and Mrs. Haug, Mrs. Carlson, Miss Clapp, Miss Auforth, Miss Greig, Mrs. Deckelman, Mrs. Bennett, Mrs. Bissell, Mrs. Wright, Mr. Roberts, Mr. Reed, Mrs. Reed, Miss Dean, Miss Briggs, Mrs. Bickhart, and Ernest Kopp.

In 1917, the American Bahá'ís celebrated a "Centennial Festival" to commemorate the one-hundredth anniversary of the birth of Bahá'u'lláh. This photograph was taken at the opening banquet held in the evening on Saturday, November 10, in the Banquet Hall, on the ninth floor of the Auditorium Hotel in Chicago.

On the following Sunday morning, there was an exhibition of moving pictures of 'Abdu'l-Bahá in America which was narrated by Albert Windust. Zia Bagdadi then showed stereoscopic scenes of the Holy Land. On Sunday afternoon, there was a public meeting in the hotel.

Monday began with a commemorative meeting on the Mashriqu'l-Adhkár site, followed by a program at the hotel. In the afternoon there was a convention on teaching, and in the evening the celebrations finished with a series of talks on the Mashriqu'l-Adhkár. All the meetings in the hotel were held in the same room as the opening banquet.

Along the back wall in the photograph, one can see an exhibit of suggested Mashriqu'l-Adhkár designs by Charles Mason Remey that was kept on display throughout the centenary celebrations and about which he gave a talk on Monday evening. Some of these designs were among those shown in New York in 1920, when a design by Louis Bourgeois was finally chosen as the basis for the Wilmette building.

CENTENNIAL CELEBRATION
OF THE BIRTH OF
BAHA'O'LLAH
Auditorium Hotel   Nov. 10,1917
Chicago, Ills.

This idyllic scene shows a group of Bahá'ís enjoying each other's company in a sun-dappled wood in Van Cortland Park, New York, in 1918. At the left are Della Lincoln, Mrs. Lincoln, and Mrs. Kelsey. The boy pointing his camera at the photographer is Robert Kelsey. At the right are Howard Colby Ives and Curtis Kelsey. The Kelseys were a notable Bahá'í family, and Curtis would become well known as an author. Ives was the author of *Portals to Freedom* and a noted Bahá'í teacher. A copy of *Tablets of Abdul Baha* is prominently displayed at the center of the scene.

On the evening of November 26, 1918, the Chicago Bahá'ís celebrated the Day of the Covenant in the Grill Hall of the Stevens Building on Wabash Avenue. Around one-hundred people attended. As the World War had just ended and communication with 'Abdu'l-Bahá had just recently been restored, there was an especially hopeful feeling to this celebration. Everyone hoped that 'Abdu'l-Bahá might visit America again. There was a selection of readings from Bahá'u'lláh's writings, including from the Kitáb-i Aqdas, on the subject of the Covenant and the station of 'Abdu'l-Bahá, interspersed with chanting by Zeenat Bagdadi. Zia Bagdadi (seated, right) sang a song in praise of 'Abdu'l-Bahá from the repertoire of the Bahá'í students at Beirut College.

Though it may not be immediately obvious from this photograph, it was a matter of pride that a large number of African-Americans attended this celebration. This interracial gathering was seen as typical of the ability of Bahá'í events to unite people. Sadly, such united social occasions were rare in Chicago. The city was torn by vicious race riots the following year during which some of the Bahá'ís distinguished themselves by hiding people fleeing from the mob.

Feast of the Center of the Covenant
ABDUL BAHA
Nov. 26, 1919

From 1917 there was increased interest in Bahá'í children's activities and many communities organized groups of "Bahai Juniors." This photograph of some of the Boston "Juniors" was taken in 1920. The woman standing on the right at the back is Ella Robarts. She edited and published *The Children of the Kingdom* which was one of a few magazines that provided information about, and material to support, such Bahá'í children's programs. Also in the photograph is Mrs. Oglesby who, with her husband, was asked by 'Abdu'l-Bahá to advocate for racial unity in the United States.

Fortunatcly, we know the names of almost everyone in this delightful group. In the back row (left to right) are: Ashley King, Rachel Small, Bahai Billy Randall, Leonora Holsapple, Aziz Badi Ober, Bahiyyih Margaret Randall, Mrs. Oglesby, Norman King, and Ella Robarts.

In the front row (left to right) are: Muriel King, unknown, Bertha Oglesby, unknown (but he looks like one of the Mapp children), Zylpha Mapp, Benny Mapp, Janice Mapp, Richard Mapp, Frederick Barbour, and unknown.

Another publisher of Bahá'í children's material after World War I was Victoria Bedikian. In addition to magazines, she printed small pictures with Bahá'í quotations on slips of paper. They were given out in children's classes as rewards, or were used to make albums and to encourage children to learn quotations from Bahá'u'lláh and 'Abdu'l-Bahá.

Her husband was Armenian, and she was deeply concerned with the Armenian persecutions and refugee problem of this time. Many of her drawings have a somewhat Eastern European or Middle Eastern flavor that shows her desire to develop an appreciation in the United States for the cultures of that region.

She produced many small sketches like the ones reproduced here (actual size) and continued to do so well into the 1930s. Using office duplicating machine techniques, she also reproduced subtly colored drawings. "Auntie" Victoria and her drawings were known around the world and delighted several generations of Bahá'í children.

LET IT
BE IN GOD,
AND
FOR GOD!

'ABDU'L BAHÁ

HE who sows a
seed in This day
will behold his Reward
in The Fruits and
Harvest of The
Heavenly
Kingdom.

'ABDU'L BAHA
Comp Page 160

LET My Heart be dilated with
Joy by The Spirit
of Confirmat-
ion From Thy
Kingdom,
AND illum-
ine My
Sight!

Bahá'í
Scriptures.
p. 429

Teach your Children what hath been
Revealed Through The Supreme Pen, and
instruct Them what hath des-
cended From The Heaven of
Greatness and Power!

Bahá'u'lláh
Kitáb-i-Aqdás.

While the American Bahá'ís were cut off from communication with 'Abdu'l-Bahá during the war years, there occurred a number of disputes which resulted in considerable ill feeling within the community. After communication with the Holy Land was restored, 'Abdu'l-Bahá encouraged the Bahá'ís to come together and to forget previous quarrels.

In 1920, 'Abdu'l-Bahá sent Jenabe Fazel Mazandarani to the United States to attend the annual Bahai Temple Unity convention and to tour the country and help reunify the community. This photograph was taken by "flashlight" at a reception for Jenabe Fazel hosted by Agnes Parsons in Washington, D.C., in June, 1920. The picture shows how his visit encouraged the Bahá'ís to reach out and to embrace the diversity in their community, rather than dwell on divisions and disagreements.

Jenabe Fazel is seated in the front row and is easily distinguished by his white headgear. To his right is his interpreter, Manucher Khan. Agnes Parsons is seated on his left.

Talk by 'Abdu'l-Bahá

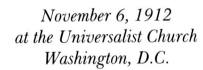

November 6, 1912
at the Universalist Church
Washington, D.C.

Notes by Joseph H. Hannen

Praise be to God! The standard of liberty is held aloft in this land. You enjoy political liberty; you enjoy liberty of thought and speech, religious liberty, racial and personal liberty. Surely this is worthy of appreciation and thanksgiving. In this connection let me mention the freedom, hospitality and universal welcome extended to me during my recent travels throughout America. I wish also to reciprocate fully and completely the warm greeting and friendly attitude of the revered doctor, pastor of this church, whose loving and quickened susceptibilities especially command acknowledgment. Surely men who are leaders of thought must conform to the example of his kindliness and goodwill. Liberalism is essential in this day—justness and equity toward all nations and people. Human attitudes must not be limited; for God is unlimited, and whosoever is the servant of the threshold of God must, likewise, be free from limitations. The world of existence is an emanation of the merciful attribute of God. God has shone forth upon the phenomena of being through His effulgence of mercy, and He is clement and kind to all His creation. Therefore, the world of humanity must ever be the recipient of bounties from His majesty, the eternal Lord, even as Christ has declared, "Be ye therefore perfect, even as your Father which is in heaven is perfect." For His bounties, like the light and heat of the sun in the material heavens, descend alike upon all mankind. Consequently, man must learn the lesson of kindness and beneficence from God Himself. Just as God is kind to all humanity, man also must be kind to his fellow creatures. If his attitude is just and loving toward his fellowmen, toward all creation, then indeed is he worthy of being pronounced the image and likeness of God.

Brotherhood, or fraternity, is of different kinds. It may be family association, the intimate relationship of the household. This is limited and subject to change and disruption. How often it happens that in a family love and agreement are changed into enmity and antagonism. Another form of fraternity is manifest in patriotism. Man loves his fellowmen because they belong to the same native land. This is also limited and subject to change and disintegration as, for instance, when sons of the same fatherland are opposed to each other in war, bloodshed and battle. Still another brotherhood, or fraternity, is that which arises from racial unity, the oneness of racial origin, producing ties of affinity and association. This, likewise, has its limitation and liability to change, for often war and deadly strife have been witnessed between people and nations of the same racial lineage. There is a fourth kind of brotherhood, the attitude of man toward humanity itself, the altruistic love of humankind and recognition of the fundamental human bond. Although this is unlimited, it is, nevertheless, susceptible to change and destruction. Even from this universal fraternal bond the looked-for result does not appear. What is the looked-for result? Loving-kindness among all human creatures and a firm, indestructible brotherhood which includes all the divine possibilities and significances in humanity. Therefore, it is evident that fraternity, love and kindness based upon family, native land, race or an attitude of altruism are neither sufficient nor permanent since all of them are limited, restricted and liable to change and disruption. For in the family there is discord and alienation; among the sons of the same fatherland, strife and internecine warfare are witnessed; between those of a given race, hostility and hatred are frequent; and even among the altruists, varying aspects of opinion and lack of unselfish devotion give little promise of permanent and indestructible unity among mankind.

Therefore, the Lord of mankind has caused His holy, divine Manifestations to come into the world. He has revealed His heavenly Books in order to establish spiritual brotherhood and through the power of the Holy Spirit has made it practicable for perfect fraternity to be realized among mankind. And when through the breaths of the Holy Spirit this perfect fraternity and agreement are established amongst men—this brotherhood and love being spiritual in character, this loving-kindness being heavenly, these constraining bonds being divine—a unity appears which is indissoluble, unchanging and never subject to transformation. It is ever the same and will forever remain the same. For example, consider the foundation of the brotherhood laid by Christ. Observe how that fraternity was conducive to unity and accord and how it brought various souls to a plane of uniform attainment where they were willing to sacrifice their lives for each other. They were content to renounce possessions and ready to forfeit joyously life itself. They lived together in such love and fellowship that even Galen, the famous Greek philosopher who was not a Christian, in his work entitled "The Progress of the Nations" said that religious beliefs are greatly conducive to the foundation of real civilization. As a proof thereof he said, "A certain number of people contemporaneous with us are known as Christians. These enjoy the superlative degree of moral civilization. Each one of them is as a great philosopher because they live together in the utmost love and good fellowship. They sacrifice life for each other. They offer worldly possessions for each other. You can say of the Christian people that they are as one person. There is a bond amongst them that is indissoluble in character."

It is evident, therefore, that the foundation of real brotherhood, the cause of loving cooperation and reciprocity and the source of real kindness and unselfish devotion is none other than the breaths of the Holy Spirit. Without this influence and animus it is impossible. We may be able to realize some degrees of fraternity through other motives, but these are limited associations and subject to change. When human brotherhood is founded upon the Holy Spirit, it is eternal, changeless, unlimited.

In various parts of the Orient there was a time when brotherhood, loving-kindness and all the praiseworthy qualities of mankind seemed to have disappeared. There was no evidence of patriotic, religious or racial fraternity; but conditions of bigotry, hatred and prejudice prevailed instead. The adherents of each religion were violent enemies of the others, filled with the spirit of hostility and eager for shedding of blood. The present war in the Balkans furnishes a parallel of these conditions. Consider the bloodshed, ferocity and oppression manifested there even in this enlightened century—all of it based fundamentally upon religious prejudice and disagreement. For the nations involved belong to the same races and native lands; nevertheless, they are savage and merciless toward each other.

Similar deplorable conditions prevailed in Persia in the nineteenth century. Darkness and ignorant fanaticism were widespread; no trace of fellowship or brotherhood existed amongst the races. On the contrary, human hearts were filled with rage and hatred; darkness and gloom were manifest in human lives and conditions everywhere. At such a time as this Bahá'u'lláh appeared upon the divine horizon, even as the glory of the sun, and in that gross darkness and hopelessness of the human world there shone a great light. He founded the oneness of the world of humanity, declaring that all mankind are as sheep and that God is the real and true Shepherd. The Shepherd is one, and all people are of His flock.

The world of humanity is one, and God is equally kind to all. What, then, is the source of unkindness and hatred in the human world? This real Shepherd loves all His sheep. He leads them in green pastures. He rears and protects them. What, then, is the source of enmity and alienation among humankind? Whence this conflict and strife? The real underlying cause is lack of religious unity and association, for in each of the great religions we find superstition, blind imitation of creeds, and theological formulas adhered to instead of the divine fundamentals, causing difference and divergence among mankind instead of agreement and fellowship. Consequently, strife, hatred and warfare have arisen, based upon this divergence and separation. If we investigate the foundations of the divine religions, we find them to be one, absolutely changeless and never subject to transformation. For example, each of the divine religions contains two kinds of laws or ordinances. One division concerns the world of morality and ethical institutions. These are the essential ordinances. They instill and awaken the knowledge and love of God, love for humanity, the virtues of the world of mankind, the attributes of the divine Kingdom, rebirth and resurrection from the kingdom of nature. These constitute one kind of divine law which is common to all and never subject to change. From the dawn of the Adamic cycle to the present day this fundamental law of God has continued changeless. This is the foundation of divine religion.

The second division comprises laws and institutions which provide for human needs and conditions according to exigencies of time and place. These are accidental, of no essential importance and should never have been made the cause and source of human contention. For example, during the time of Moses—upon Him be peace!—according to the exigencies of that period, divorce was permissible. During the cycle of Christ, inasmuch as divorce was not in conformity with the time and conditions, Jesus Christ abrogated it. In the cycle of Moses plurality of wives was permissible. But during the time of Christ the exigency which had sanctioned it did not exist; therefore, it was forbidden. Moses lived in the wilderness and desert of Sinai; therefore, His ordinances and commandments were in conformity with those conditions. The penalty for theft was to cut of a man's hand. An ordinance of this kind was in keeping with desert life but is not compatible with conditions of the present day. Such ordinances, therefore, constitute the second or nonessential division of the divine religions and are not of importance, for they deal with human transactions which are ever changing according to the requirements of time and place. Therefore, the intrinsic foundations of the divine religions are one. As this is true, why should hostility and strife exist among them? Why should this hatred and warfare, ferocity and bloodshed continue? Is this allowable and justified? God forbid!

An essential principle of Bahá'u'lláh's teaching is that religion must be the cause of unity and love amongst men; that it is the supreme effulgence of Divinity, the stimulus of life, the source of honor and productive of eternal existence. Religion is not intended to arouse enmity and hatred nor to become the source of tyranny and injustice. Should it prove to be the cause of hostility, discord and the alienation of mankind, assuredly the absence of religion would be preferable. Religious teachings are like a course of treatment having for its purpose the cure and healing of mankind. If the only outcome of a course of treatment should be mere diagnosis and fruitless discussion of symptoms, it would be better to abandon and abolish it. In this sense the absence of religion would be at least some progress toward unity.

Furthermore, religion must conform to reason and be in accord with the conclusions of science. For religion, reason and science are realities; therefore, these three, being realities, must conform and be reconciled. A question or principle which is religious in its nature must be sanctioned by science. Science must declare it to be valid, and reason must confirm it in order that it may inspire confidence. If religious teaching, however, be at variance with science and reason, it is unquestionably superstition. The Lord of mankind has bestowed upon us the faculty of reason whereby we may discern the realities of things. How then can man rightfully accept any proposition which is not in conformity with the processes of reason and the principles of science? Assuredly such a course cannot inspire man with confidence and real belief.

The teachings of Bahá'u'lláh embody many principles; I am giving you only a synopsis. One of these principles concerns equality between men and women. He declared that as all are created in the image and likeness of the one God, there is no distinction as to sex in the estimation of God. He who is purest in heart, whose knowledge exceeds and who excels in kindness to the servants of God, is nearest and dearest to the Lord, our Creator, irrespective of sex. In the lower kingdoms, the animal and vegetable, we find sex differentiation in function and organism. All plants, trees and animals are subject to that differentiation by creation, but among themselves there is absolute equality without further distinction as to sex. Why, then, should mankind make a distinction which the lower creatures do not regard? Especially so when we realize that all are of the same kingdom and kindred; that all are the leaves of one tree, the waves of one sea? The only reasonable explanation is that woman has not been afforded the same educational facilities as man. For if she had received the same opportunities for training and development as man has enjoyed, undoubtedly she would have attained the same station and level. On the estimate of God no distinction exists; both are as one and possess equal degrees of capacity. Therefore, through opportunity and development woman will merit and attain the same prerogatives. When Jesus Christ died upon the cross, the disciples who witnessed His crucifixion were disturbed and shaken. Even Peter, one of the greatest of His followers, denied Him thrice. Mary Magdalene brought them together and confirmed their faith, saying, "Why are ye doubting? Why have ye feared? O thou Peter! Why didst thou deny Him? For Christ was not crucified. The reality of Christ is ever-living, everlasting, eternal. For that divine reality there is no beginning, no ending, and, therefore, there can be no death. At most, only the body of Jesus has suffered death." In brief, this woman, singly and alone, was instrumental in transforming the disciples and making them steadfast. This is an evidence of extraordinary power and supreme attributes, a proof that woman is the equivalent and complement of man. The one who is better trained and educated, whose aptitude is greater and whose ideals are higher is most distinguished and worthy—whether man or woman.

Through the teachings of Bahá'u'lláh the horizon of the East was made radiant and glorious. Souls who have hearkened to His words and accepted His message live together today in complete fellowship and love. They even offer their lives for each other. They forego and renounce worldly possessions for one another, each preferring the other to himself. This has been due to the declaration and foundation of the oneness of the world of humanity. Today in Persia there are meetings and assemblages wherein souls who have become illumined by the teachings of Bahá'u'lláh—representative Muslims, Christians, Jews, Zoroastrians, Buddhists and of the various denominations of each—mingle and conjoin in perfect fellowship and absolute agreement. A wonderful brotherhood and love is established among them, and all are united in spirit and service for international peace. More than twenty thousand Bahá'ís have given their lives in martyrdom for the Cause of God. The governments of the East arose against them, bent upon their extermination. They were killed relentlessly, but day by day their numbers have increased, day by day they have multiplied in strength and become more eloquent. They have been strengthened through the efficacy of a wonderful spiritual power. How savage and fearful the ferocity of man against his fellowman! Consider what is taking place now in the Balkans, what blood is being shed. Even the wild beasts and ferocious animals do not commit such acts. The most ferocious wolf kills but one sheep a day, and even that for his food. But now in the Balkans one man destroys ten fellow beings. The commanders of armies glory in having killed ten thousand men, not for food, nay, rather, for military control, territorial greed, fame and possession of the dust of the earth. They kill for national aggrandizement, notwithstanding this terrestrial globe is but a dark world of grossest matter. It is a world of sorrow and grief, a world of disappointment and unhappiness, a world of death. For after all, the earth is but the everlasting graveyard, the vast, universal cemetery of all mankind. Yet men fight to possess this graveyard, waging war and battle, killing each other. What ignorance! How spacious the earth is with room in plenty for all! How thoughtful the providence which has so allotted that every man may derive his sustenance from it! The Lord, our Creator, does not ordain that anyone should starve or live in want. All are intended to participate in the blessed and abundant bestowals of our God. Fundamentally, all warfare and bloodshed in the human world are due to the lack of unity between the religions, which through superstitions and adherence to theological dogmas have obscured the one reality which is the source and basis of them all.

As to the American people: This noble nation, intelligent, thoughtful, reflective, is not impelled by motives of territorial aggrandizement and lust for domination. Its boundaries are insular and geographically separated from the other nations. Here we find a oneness of interest and unity of national policy. These are, indeed, United States. Therefore, this nation possesses the capacity and capability for holding aloft the banner of international peace. May this noble people be the cause of unifying humanity. May they spread broadcast the heavenly civilization and illumination, become the cause of the diffusion of the love of God, proclaim the solidarity of mankind and be the cause of the guidance of the human race. Therefore, I ask that you will give this all-important question your most serious consideration and efforts. May the world of humanity find peace and composure and this dark earth be transformed into a realm of radiance. May the East and West clasp hands together. May the oneness of God become reflected and fully revealed in the hearts of humanity and all mankind prove to be the manifestations of the favors of God.

Necessarily there will be some who are defective amongst men, but it is our duty to enable them by kind methods of guidance and teaching to become perfected. Some will be found who are morally sick; they should be treated in order that they may be healed. Others are immature and like children; they must be trained and educated so that they may become wise and mature. Those who are asleep must be awakened; the indifferent must become mindful and attentive. But all this must be accomplished in the spirit of kindness and love and not by strife, antagonism nor in a spirit of hostility and hatred, for this is contrary to the good pleasure of God. That which is acceptable in the sight of God is love. Love is, in reality, the first effulgence of Divinity and the greatest splendor of God.

O Thou compassionate Lord, Thou Who art generous and able! We are servants of Thine sheltered beneath Thy providence. Cast Thy glance of favor upon us. Give light to our eyes, hearing to our ears, and understanding and love to our hearts. Render our souls joyous and happy through Thy glad tidings. O Lord! Point out to us the pathway of Thy kingdom and resuscitate all of us through the breaths of the Holy Spirit. Bestow upon us life everlasting and confer upon us never-ending honor. Unify mankind and illumine the world of humanity. May we all follow Thy pathway, long for Thy good pleasure and seek the mysteries of Thy kingdom. O God! Unite us and connect our hearts with Thine indissoluble bond. Verily, Thou art the Giver, Thou art the Kind One and Thou art the Almighty.

Sources for Quotations

p. 1: *Selections from the Writings of ‘Abdu’l-Bahá* (Haifa: Bahá’í World Centre, 1978) p. 243.

p. 24: *The Diary of Juliet Thompson* (Los Angeles: Kalimát Press, 1983) p. 323.

p. 26: *The Promulgation of Universal Peace* (Wilmette, Ill.: Bahá’í Publishing Trust, 1982) p. 328.

p. 30: *Promulgation*, pp. 343-44.

p. 46: *Selections*, p. 244-45.

pp. 126-35: *Promulgation*, pp. 390-97.

R. Jackson Armstrong-Ingram is an archivist at the Nevada State Library and Archives and a cultural anthropologist with a particular interest in cross-cultural contact. He is the author of Music, Devotions & Mashriqu'l-Adhkár, *Volume Four of the* Studies in the Babí and Bahá'í Religions Series, *also published by Kalimát Press.*